I See Triangles

D.H. Dilkes

Bailey Books
an imprint of
Enslow Publishers, Inc.
40 Industrial Road
Box 398
Berkeley Heights, NJ 07922
USA
http://www.enslow.com

Bailey Books, an imprint of Enslow Publishers, Inc.

Library of Congress Cataloging-in-Publication Data

Dilkes, D. H.
 I see triangles / by D.H. Dilkes.
  p. cm. — (All about shapes)
 Includes index.
 Summary: "Simple text and photographs present a story with a theme about
triangles"—Provided by publisher.
 ISBN 978-0-7660-3804-2
 1. Triangle—Juvenile literature. 2. Shapes—Juvenile literature. I. Title.
 QA482.D54 2011
 516'.154—dc22

                                    2010018424

Paperback ISBN: 978-1-59845-155-9

Printed in the United States of America

052010 Lake Book Manufacturing, Inc., Melrose Park, IL

10 9 8 7 6 5 4 3 2 1

To Our Readers: We have done our best to make sure all Internet Addresses in this
book were active and appropriate when we went to press. However, the author and the
publisher have no control over and assume no liability for the material available on those
Internet sites or on other Web sites they may link to. Any comments or suggestions can
be sent by e-mail to comments@enslow.com or to the address on the back cover.

♻ Enslow Publishers, Inc., is committed to printing our books on recycled paper.
The paper in every book contains 10% to 30% post-consumer waste (PCW). The cover
board on the outside of each book contains 100% PCW. Our goal is to do our part to help
young people and the environment too!

Note to Parents and Teachers

Help pre-readers get a jumpstart on reading. These lively stories introduce simple
concepts with repetition of words and short simple sentences. Photos and illustrations fill
the pages with color and effectively enhance the text. Free Educator Guides are available
for this series at www.enslow.com. Search for the *All About Shapes* series name.

Contents

Words to Know

blue

street

triangle

I see triangles.

Do you?

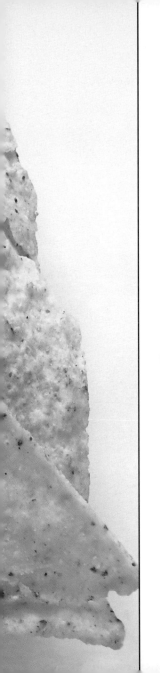

Some I can eat,

one that is blue.

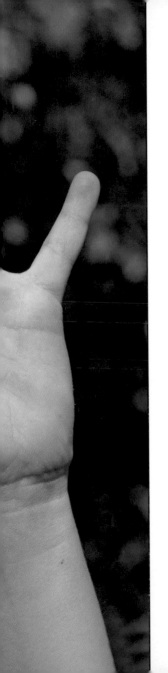

One I can make.

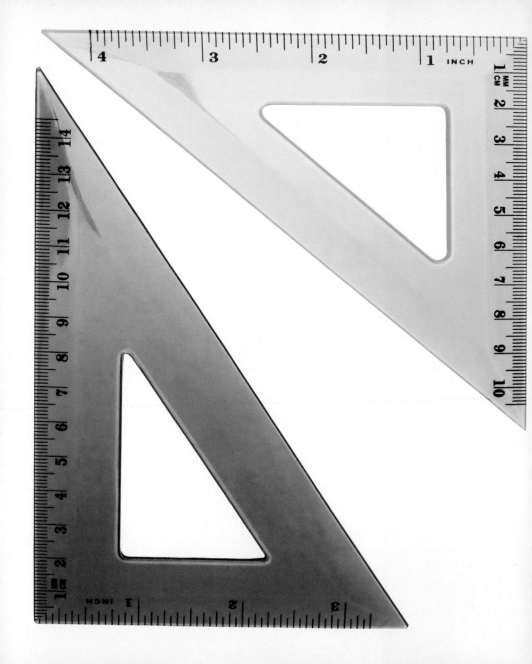

Is this more than two?

One is by a street.

17

One my dog gets into.

Many I can eat!

I can play a triangle.
Can you?

Read More

Jones, Christianne C. *Party of Three: A Book About Triangles.* Minneapolis, Minn.: Picture Window Books, 2006.

Lorbiecki, Marybeth. *Triangles.* Edina, Minn.: Magic Wagon, 2008.

Web Sites

Fisher-Price. *Learn Your Colors and Shapes.*
<http://www.fisher-price.com/us/fun/games/colorshapes/>
Press any key to start!

Kids Learning Station. *Preschool Shapes Worksheets.*
<http://www.kidslearningstation.com/preschool/shapes
-worksheets.asp>
Click on "Triangles Worksheet."

Index

Guided Reading Level: B
Guided Reading Leveling System is based on the guidelines
recommended by Fountas and Pinnell.

Word Count: 43